PHYSICAL
SCIENCE
PROJECTS
★ for Kids ★

A PROJECT GUIDE TO

SOUND

Colleen Kessler

Mitchell Lane

P.O. Box 196
Hockessin, Delaware 19707
Visit us on the web: www.mitchelllane.com
Comments? email us: mitchelllane@mitchelllane.com

Mitchell Lane

PHYSICAL
SCIENCE
PROJECTS
☆ For Kids ☆

A Project Guide to:
Chemistry • Electricity and Magnetism
Forces and Motion • Light and Optics
Matter • **Sound**

PUBLISHER'S NOTE: The facts on which this book is based have been thoroughly researched. Documentation of such research can be found on page 44. While every possible effort has been made to ensure accuracy, the publisher will not assume liability for damages caused by inaccuracies in the data, and makes no warranty on the accuracy of the information contained herein.

The Internet sites referenced herein were active as of the publication date. Due to the fleeting nature of some web sites, we cannot guarantee they will all be active when you are reading this book.

To reflect current usage, we have chosen to use the secular era designations BCE ("before the common era") and CE ("of the common era") instead of the traditional designations BC ("before Christ") and AD (*anno Domini*, "in the year of the Lord").

**Library of Congress
Cataloging-in-Publication Data**

Kessler, Colleen D.
 A project guide to sound / Colleen D. Kessler.
    p. cm. — (Physical science projects for kids)
 Includes bibliographical references and index.
 ISBN 978-1-58415-970-4 (library bound)
 1. Sound—Juvenile literature. I. Title.
 QC225.5.K395 2011
 534—dc22
                                                    2011012532

eBook ISBN: 9781612281124

PLB

Printing   1   2   3   4   5   6   7   8   9

CONTENTS

Sound waves

INTRODUCTION

Music plays, birds sing, car horns honk, dogs bark, your little sister screams . . . sound is all around you. Where does it come from? How is it made? How do we hear it?

All sounds are created when something vibrates, or moves quickly back and forth. Vibrations create waves, which are a form of energy. Have you ever watched the string of a guitar after it has been plucked? When it moves back and forth, waves travel through the air around the guitar string. You hear those waves as a tone. A tone is a steady sound with even wavelengths.

Greek philosopher Pythagoras studied vibrations in the sixth century BCE. Then, in the fourth century BCE, Aristotle suggested that sound must be carried through a medium such as air or water. He predicted that it could not travel in a vacuum (an area in which there is nothing, not even air). In 1660, Irish scientist Robert Boyle proved that this was true. Sound could not travel in a vacuum.

Sound waves spread out in all directions from their source. When they reach your ear, they cause your eardrum to vibrate. The vibrations are processed in your brain as sound.

There are four main parts to a sound wave. The wavelength is the measurement of one up-and-down cycle of a wave. A cycle has one area of increased pressure (waves are closer together) and one area of lower pressure (waves are farther apart). The period of a wave is the time it takes for one complete cycle of a wave to pass a certain point.

The amplitude of a sound wave is determined by the height of the wave. Loud sounds have high amplitudes. Soft sounds have low amplitudes. A decibel is the unit that scientists use to measure loudness. The softest sounds that humans can hear measure zero decibels. People usually talk at 60 decibels.

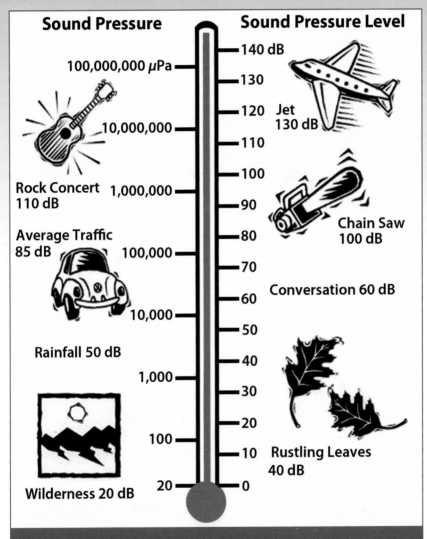

Loudness is measured in decibels (dB). A running jet engine is louder than a falling leaf, so it is measured at a higher decibel level than the leaf. Sound pressure is how much the sound vibrations compress air. It is measured in micropascals (µPa).

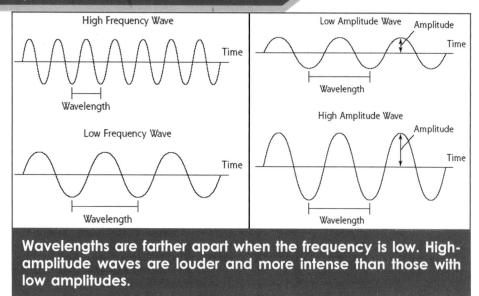

Wavelengths are farther apart when the frequency is low. High-amplitude waves are louder and more intense than those with low amplitudes.

Finally, the frequency of a wave is the number of cycles a wave makes per second as it passes a specific location. Frequencies are measured in hertz (Hz). Your brain interprets the frequency of a sound wave as pitch. The faster the vibrations are, the higher the pitch is. When frequency is low, and vibrations are slow, the pitch is low. You can see and hear this when you pluck a guitar string. Longer strings vibrate slower than shorter strings. If a string is left open and plucked,

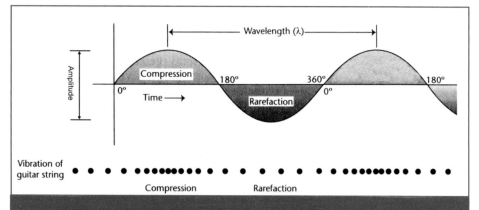

In this diagram, the compressions (where particles are crowded together) appear as an upward curve on the line. The rarefactions (where particles are spread apart) appear as the downward curve of the line. The wavelength is the distance between the crest of one wave and the crest of another.

the sound is low. If you press the string against the neck of the guitar to make it shorter, the sound is higher.

The speed of sound is much slower than the speed of light. This is why we see lightning before we hear the boom of thunder caused by it. Sound travels at different speeds depending on the medium through which it is traveling. Of the three main states of matter (liquid, solid, and gas), sound waves move the quickest through solids. They move slowest through gases.

The modern study of sound, called acoustics, began in the early 1600s with French scientist Marin Mersenne and Italian scientist Galileo Galilei. Mersenne is sometimes referred to as the "father of acoustics,"

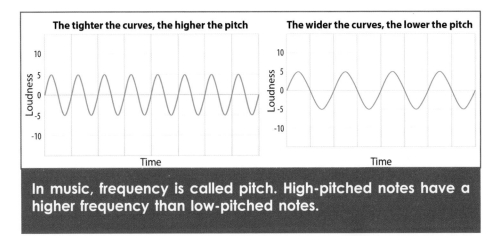

The tighter the curves, the higher the pitch

The wider the curves, the lower the pitch

In music, frequency is called pitch. High-pitched notes have a higher frequency than low-pitched notes.

though both he and Galileo came up with detailed theories about frequencies and the movements of sound waves.

As early scientists discovered, solid objects do not stop sound waves. The waves can simply bend around them (diffract) or bounce off them (reflect).

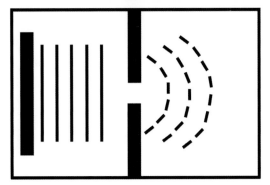

Sound waves bend, or diffract, around solid walls.

Imagine that you have music playing loudly in your room with the door open. The sound waves will go through the opening easily, but they will slow down as they pass the frame of the door. This makes them bend around the walls on the other side of the opening. If sound waves did not diffract, you would only be able to hear the music if you stood directly in front of the open door. Instead, the sound waves spread out in a semicircle from the open doorway. If you stand in front of the door, you hear the sound the loudest. If you move to either side, the sound you hear will be softer.

Understanding sound and its wave properties has allowed scientists to develop many exciting types of technology. People can usually hear sound frequencies between 20 and 20,000 hertz. When a wave's frequency is above 20,000 hertz, it is called ultrasonic. We use ultrasonic waves to perform ultrasounds, in sonar, and in cleaning services, among other things.

Your mother may have had an ultrasound performed so that doctors could look at you before you were born. Maybe you know someone who has had an ultrasound image taken of his or her liver, bladder, or other organ to help doctors determine what was wrong.

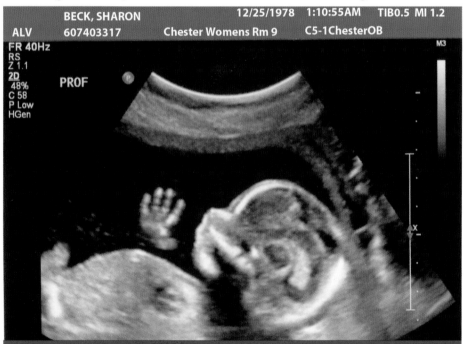

BECK, SHARON   607403317   12/25/1978 1:10:55AM   TIB0.5 MI 1.2
ALV   Chester Womens Rm 9   C5-1ChesterOB
FR 40Hz
RS
Z 1.1
2D
48%   PROF
C 58
P Low
HGen
M3

To make a sonogram of an unborn baby, harmless ultrasonic waves are sent through the mother's womb. The sound waves bounce off solid objects (the baby), and the reflected waves create a picture.

Ultrasound images, called sonograms, use sound waves in the same way bats and dolphins use them to find food. In nature, this is called echolocation. These animals send out sound waves that bounce back to them. This helps them form a picture of where prey is located.

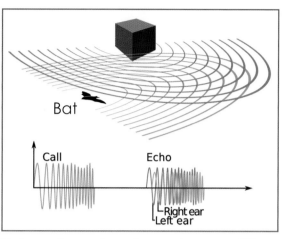

Bats emit a series of sound waves. When these waves bounce off an object and back to the bat, the bat can tell where the object is and whether it is moving.

Sonar stands for SOund NAvigation Ranging. It is used to help navigate, to track storms and ships, and to direct missiles. To track aircraft, for example, a transmitter sends ultrasonic sound waves up into the air. These waves bounce off the aircraft and return to a receiver, which records the location of the plane.

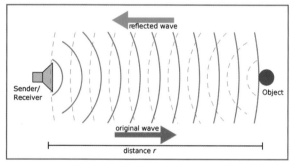

Principle of an active sonar

The activities and experiments in this book will introduce you to many applications of the physics of sound. For each experiment, be sure to read all the directions before you begin. Keep a science notebook. This can serve as a record of the activities and experiments you have completed, and can be used as a springboard for you to create your own investigations. If an activity suggests that you perform it with an adult, be sure to do so. Most important, use common sense. If you follow directions and safety tips, you'll have a good time AND learn something about the sounds that surround you every day!

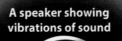

A speaker showing vibrations of sound

SALT DRUM

As you learned in the introduction, sound is created when something vibrates, or moves back and forth. Sound waves are created because the air around a vibrating object begins to vibrate, too. These vibrations travel through the air and get picked up by our ears as sounds.

You can't really see sound waves as they travel, but you can see the effects of those waves. In this activity, you'll observe the effects of sound waves on a simple drum. Watch the salt "dance" as the waves hit it!

Materials
- Empty margarine tub or bowl
- Plastic wrap
- Rubber band
- Salt
- Two empty plastic bottles

Instructions
1. Cover the top of an empty margarine tub or bowl with a tight layer of plastic wrap.
2. Secure it with a rubber band.

Move the bottles closer to and farther from the salt to get different results.

3. Sprinkle salt over the top of your drum.
4. Bang the empty water bottles together above the drum. Watch the salt "dance" as the sound waves hit it.
5. Hold the bottles closer to the drum when you hit them together. Do you notice a difference in the way the salt moves? How about if you hold them farther away when you hit them together?

When you hit the bottles together, the impact makes a sound. The waves created by that sound spread out and make the salt move.

HUMAN HEARING

Humans hear because of a different type of drum: the eardum. The human ear is made up of three parts: the outer ear, the middle ear, and the inner ear. The outer ear, or auricle, is the part that people see. This part is responsible for collecting sounds. It acts kind of like a funnel. It directs sounds into the ear canal.

The eardrum is a thin membrane that separates the outer ear from the middle ear. When sound waves reach the eardrum, they make it vibrate. These vibrations cause the three tiniest bones in your body—the malleus (hammer), incus (anvil), and stapes (stirrup)—to vibrate too. Their vibrations send sound waves along to the inner ear, or cochlea (KOH-klee-uh). The cochlea is filled with fluid, and it is lined with thousands of tiny hairs. The hairs change the vibrations to signals that tell the brain what it is hearing.

In this activity, you'll use different colored clay to create a model of the human ear. Follow the colors to see where the sound takes you!

Materials
- Ear diagram (on page 13)
- Seven different colors of modeling clay or dough
- Glue

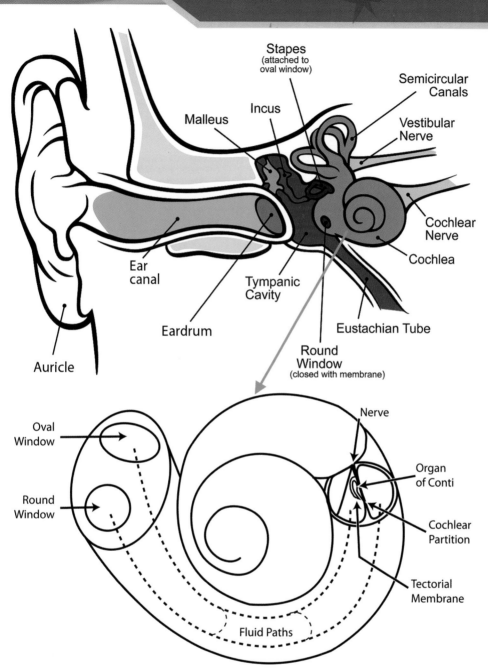

In humans, sound enters the auricle and travels down the ear canal, making the eardrum vibrate. The vibrations set the tiny ear bones in motion, which send sound waves into the cochlea. The cochlea is filled with fluid. Sound waves travel through the fluid from the oval window to the cochlear partition and back. On the way, tiny hairs turn these waves into electrical impulses that the brain can decode as sounds.

Instructions

1. Choose one color of the clay. Roll this into a 6-inch-long snake, about ¼-inch wide, and shape it into a coil. Leave a small amount (about ½ inch) of the clay extended to connect to the rest of your ear. This coil is the cochlea.

2. Choose another color of clay and form several loops. These will be the semicircular canals and should be about the size of the cochlea. This is the part of your ear that helps you stay balanced. In fact, if you get an infection in your semicircular canals, you won't be able to stand up!

3. Using a new clay color, form the malleus, incus, and stapes. These "bones" should be very small.

4. Mold an eardrum using a different color.

5. Choose a color for the Eustachian tube. Roll one section of this color flat, and the other into a two-inch snake.

6. Using the diagram for guidance, arrange the bones and semicircular canals on top of the flat Eustachian tube.

7. Attach the cochlea, the rest of the Eustachian tube, and the eardrum.

8. With another color, form a snake to make the ear canal.

9. Use the final color to mold the outer ear. Attach the ear canal to the eardrum and the auricle.

Your model ear will allow you to trace the path sound takes as it makes its way to your brain. Paint some glue over it to preserve it.

10. Use glue as needed to make your model stiff, and let it dry overnight. You could use dots of glue where the pieces meet or you could use a paintbrush to glue all the joints—even painting over the entire object like a glaze.

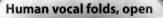

Human vocal folds, open

VOCAL VIBRATION

Humans speak when they make their vocal folds vibrate. Vocal folds are thin tissues that stretch across the trachea (windpipe). The vocal folds, along with the muscle and cartilage that support them, are called the larynx. These were once called vocal cords, but scientists now know that they are not ropy organs. Instead, they are flaps of tissue.

Your lungs blow air against these vocal folds, which open and close depending on the sound you want to make. Air pushes through the space left between them. The air makes the covering of the folds vibrate. The more air that your lungs are able to push through that opening, the louder the vibrations will be.

Reed instruments work a lot like the vocal folds. The musician squeezes the reed closer against the mouthpiece to make a higher-pitched sound, but relaxes the pressure on the reed to make a lower-

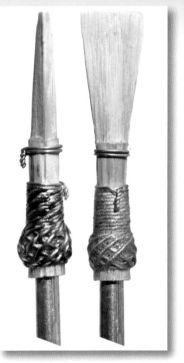

Bassoons have two reeds instead of a reed and a mouthpiece.

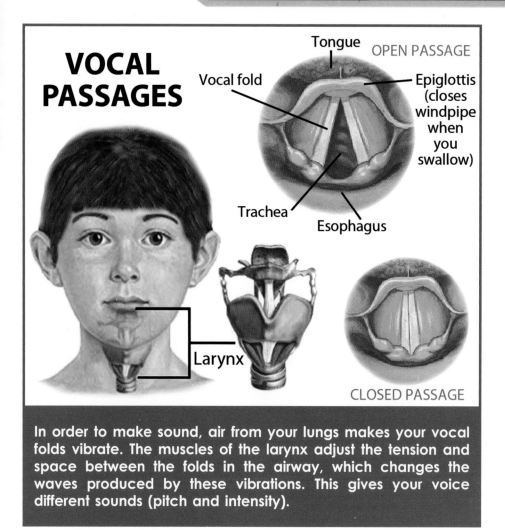

VOCAL PASSAGES

OPEN PASSAGE

Tongue

Vocal fold

Epiglottis (closes windpipe when you swallow)

Trachea

Esophagus

Larynx

CLOSED PASSAGE

In order to make sound, air from your lungs makes your vocal folds vibrate. The muscles of the larynx adjust the tension and space between the folds in the airway, which changes the waves produced by these vibrations. This gives your voice different sounds (pitch and intensity).

pitched sound. The more air the musician uses, the louder the sound. You can test these ideas using a simple straw. Then use your fingers to feel the vibrations in your larynx as you speak or sing.

Materials
♦ Straight drinking straws (without a bendable end)
♦ Scissors

Instructions
1. Bite one end of the straw to flatten it, but don't bite through it.
2. Use scissors to cut the flat end to a point.

Make sure you've flattened down your straw completely or you'll just hear blowing air.

3. Flatten the end again and blow into it. (If you hear air, flatten it some more. You should hear a buzzing sound like a kazoo.)
4. Experiment with longer and shorter straws. How does the length of your straw affect the sound that comes out of it? (Shorter straws produce higher sounds. Longer straws produce lower sounds.)

Now, put two fingers on the front part of your throat and hum a familiar song. Do you feel the vibration? This is just like the vibration of the end of the straws you just made. Press in lightly and continue humming. What happens?

When you press in, you are causing the vocal folds to become more tightly closed, so the sound becomes higher pitched.

Don't press too hard against your throat!

SOUND CANNON

When an airplane flies, it pushes airwaves ahead of it, and these spread out in all directions. Sometimes the waves move at the speed of sound, but sometimes they create faster waves, called supersonic waves. Once the airplane starts to travel faster than the speed of sound, it passes its own waves. This causes a loud disturbance—a shock wave.

Scientists measure sound waves by the number of times they make the air vibrate each second. One vibration per second is called a hertz. When you hear a sound that measures 600 hertz, the waves are hitting your eardrums at a rate of 600 times per second. In this activity, you'll use the shock waves made by a sudden disturbance of sound waves in the air to blow a sheet of tissue taped to a table. These waves won't be supersonic—we will build up to that.

Materials
- Plastic bottle
- An adult
- Scissors
- Balloon
- Rubber band
- Tissue
- Tape

19

Instructions

1. Ask an adult to cut the bottom off the plastic bottle.
2. Cut the end off the balloon, widening the opening.
3. Stretch the balloon around the bottom of the bottle so that it is tight like a drum.

4. Use the rubber band to secure the balloon to the bottle.
5. Tape the tissue to a table or chair so that it is hanging over the edge.
6. Hold the bottle a few feet away from the tissue, with the opening of the bottle facing the tissue.
7. Tap the balloon with your hand.
8. What happened to the tissue? (It should move a little.)
9. Hold the bottle farther away and tap again. Then move it closer. Experiment with different distances and taps (hard and soft). What do you notice?

The sound waves from the tap compressed the air in the bottle. The sound waves squeezed through the opening of the bottle, moving toward the tissue. Those waves were strong enough to make the tissue move, but the frequency was too low for you to hear the waves as sound. The only sound you should have heard was the tap against the balloon.

Remember, sound waves are caused when a material vibrates. In this case, the material is the balloon. The vibration of the tap against the balloon squeezes and releases the air in front of it. The air molecules squeeze and release the next layer of air. This continues until the waves of moving molecules reach the tissue. It is not air that moves from the balloon's surface to the tissue, it is the parade of moving waves caused by the sound of the balloon being tapped.

Sound waves will disturb a tissue when you tap a stretched balloon.

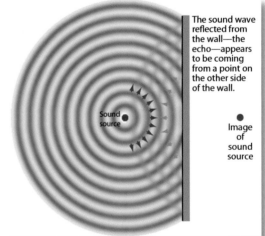

Source

Original Waves   Diffracted Waves

SOUND SHADOW

Music would be pretty boring if it all sounded the same. Instead, we hear a variety of high and low notes. This is called pitch. Pitch changes with the size of the sound waves and the speed of their vibration.

The ticking of a clock is a high-pitched sound. It is made up of short waves, which don't bend well. When you are facing something that makes a sound made up of short waves, you can hear it well because the waves are able to travel directly into your ear. When you turn away, though, the short waves are unable to bend around your head. This bending is called diffraction. Waves diffract around objects and continue moving. Sometimes sounds bounce off a solid object. This is called reflection. When they bounce back toward the source, they make an echo.

Diffraction is similar to what makes the shadows that you see on sunny days. When light from the sun is blocked

The sound wave reflected from the wall—the echo—appears to be coming from a point on the other side of the wall.

Sound source

Image of sound source

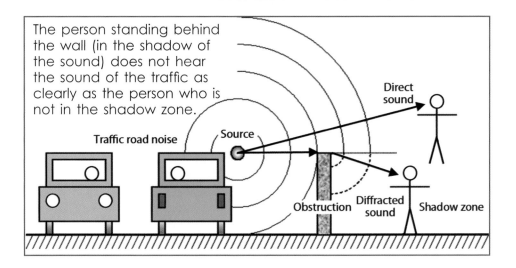

The person standing behind the wall (in the shadow of the sound) does not hear the sound of the traffic as clearly as the person who is not in the shadow zone.

Traffic road noise

Source

Direct sound

Obstruction

Diffracted sound

Shadow zone

by solid objects like trees and cars, a dark shadow is left on the side opposite the sun. A "sound shadow" happens when short sound waves are stopped before they can enter your ear. Lower-pitched sounds are made up of longer waves and can easily diffract around objects like your head.

When you see a parade, you can usually hear the marching band coming around the corner. You hear sounds like the drum because they are made up of long, low-frequency waves that diffract around the corner. Try this experiment to make a "sound shadow."

Materials
♦ Clock that ticks
♦ Table

Instructions
1. Put your clock on a table, and move about 4 or 5 feet away.
2. Face the clock. Do you hear the ticking?

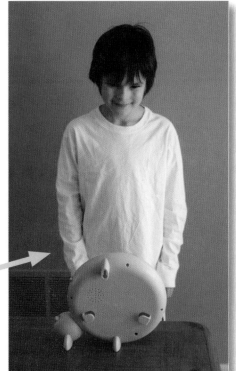

3. Gently close one of your ears with your finger. How does that change the sound?

4. Now, turn SLOWLY to the side so that your open ear is facing away from the clock. How does the sound change now?

When you are facing the clock, the ticking diffracts around your face to reach your ears. Using both of your ears, you may be able to pick up the

sound waves caused by the clock. It becomes much more difficult to hear when you use only one ear, especially if your closed ear is toward the clock. That puts your open ear in the sound shadow.

When you turn your open ear toward the clock, you can hear it easily because the sound waves travel in a straight line to your ear.

A MATTER OF SPEED

Sounds move when particles of matter bump into other particles, transferring the waves. The particles in each of the three states of matter are arranged differently. The particles in solids are very close to one another. The particles in liquids are farther apart. Gas particles are the farthest apart.

You may think that it is easier for sound to travel through the air than through a liquid. When you put your head under water, it becomes harder to hear, right? Although sound travels better through water than through air, people are not adapted to hear well underwater. When your ears are underwater, they fill up and your eardrums cannot vibrate as fast as they can in air. This makes it difficult for you to hear. Whales and dolphins, on the other hand, are adapted to hear sounds underwater. Some whales can hear sounds that have traveled across entire ocean basins.

The closer particles are to one another, the quicker sound can move. Sound moves through solids the quickest and air the slowest. Have you ever seen pictures of Native Americans with their ear to the ground? Since sound travels quickly through solid objects, they could hear approaching horses by listening to the sound through the ground.

Experiment with the three states of matter in this activity, and hear for yourself how sound travels through each.

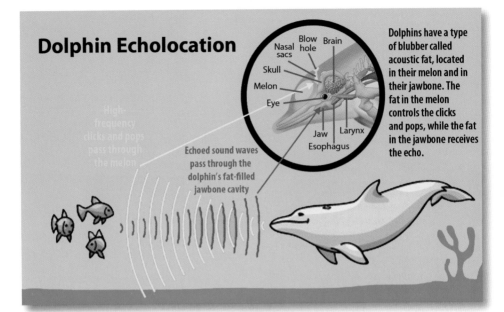

Dolphin Echolocation

High-frequency clicks and pops pass through the melon

Echoed sound waves pass through the dolphin's fat-filled jawbone cavity

Blow hole · Brain · Nasal sacs · Skull · Melon · Eye · Jaw · Larynx · Esophagus

Dolphins have a type of blubber called acoustic fat, located in their melon and in their jawbone. The fat in the melon controls the clicks and pops, while the fat in the jawbone receives the echo.

Materials
- 3 quart-size plastic zipper bags
- Sugar
- Small piece of fabric
- Water
- Table
- Spoon

Squeeze the air out of your water and sugar bags.

Instructions
1. Fill one bag halfway with water, squeeze the extra air out, and seal it tightly.
2. Fill the second bag halfway with sugar, squeeze the extra air out, and seal it tightly.
3. Fill the third bag with air and seal it carefully.
4. Set all three bags on top of the table.

5. Lay your ear on the bag of sugar and tap the table with the spoon. What do you hear?

6. Do the same thing, but listen through the bag of water. Does it sound different? The same?

7. Next, do this with your ear on the bag of air. Compare the sounds you heard.

8. Now lay your ear on a piece of fabric and tap the table with the spoon. (Do not put the fabric in a bag.) What does it sound like?

Because sound travels more quickly and easily through liquids and solids than through air, you should have been able to hear the tapping better through the bags with water and sugar than through the bag of air.

AMPLIFY IT!

When something vibrates to make a sound (like the tuning fork you will use in this activity), it also vibrates the surrounding air. If the object is small, it will not come into direct contact with very much air. The larger the surface area of an object, the more air particles it will be able to vibrate.

This is the idea behind the large speakers you see at concerts. When bands play for large crowds, they place very large speakers onstage, facing out toward the people. Big speakers have a larger vibrating surface than small speakers. As the number of vibrating air particles increases, so does the volume of the music.

In this activity, you'll use a tuning fork to demonstrate this idea. Tuning forks are quite small, so what will happen when you touch a vibrating tuning fork to an object with a larger surface area?

Materials
- Tuning fork (inexpensively available through science supply or music catalogs and at music stores)
- A large surface (such as a tabletop)

Instructions

1. Strike the tuning fork against the tabletop and hold it at arm's length. Can you hear the pitch it makes? (You should hear it faintly.)
2. Now, strike it against the table again. Quickly stand the base of its handle on the table. What is the difference in sound? (You should hear the sound get louder as the handle touches the surface of the table.)
3. Experiment with different surfaces of varying sizes and materials.

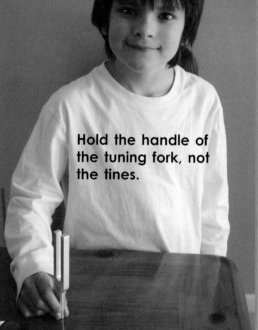

Hold the handle of the tuning fork, not the tines.

When the whole table vibrates, it disturbs more air than the tuning fork alone. The sound is louder. Different surfaces will absorb the vibrations differently, so the sounds you'll hear will have different volumes. The size differences will affect the sound as well. Sounds from smaller surfaces should be softer than those from larger surfaces of the same material.

Another Tuning Fork Experiment

Here's a quick activity you can do while you have a tuning fork handy. Have you ever heard your recorded voice? Maybe you left someone a voicemail and then listened to it. Your recorded voice sounds different to you than your normal voice, but it sounds the same to others. Why is that?

Hold the tuning fork securely against your jawbone. Try it with your mouth open and closed.

Listen to the vibrating tuning fork, then place the handle against your jaw. Does the sound change? It sounds different because of the way the sound is conducted to your ear. When you talk to someone, the sound they hear travels through the air. You hear the air particles vibrate, too, but you also hear the sounds that travel through your bones. These bone vibrations sound different than the sounds that travel through the air, so when you speak, your voice sounds different to you than it does to other people.

MOVING SOUND

Have you ever wondered why some people cup their hands around their mouth when they're yelling to someone far away? Whenever sound is concentrated, or condensed, the waves are funneled in one direction. Since they don't spread out over a large area, the sound is louder over a greater distance.

Trapping sound waves in a cup and string concentrates the vibrations. This allows the sound waves to travel farther than they would if they were spread out in the surrounding air.

As long as you keep the string on the simple "telephone" in this activity tight, you should be able to hear your friend speak.

Cup your hands around your mouth to make the sound go farther.

31

Materials
- 2 plastic cups
- An adult
- Scissors
- Measuring tape
- String
- Friend

Try your phone around corners. Try it with the string threaded under a closed door.

Instructions

1. Have an adult poke a hole in the bottom of each plastic cup.
2. Cut a five-foot length of string, and knot one end of the string tight inside each cup.
3. Give one cup to your friend.
4. Stand apart so that the string is tight.
5. Have your friend speak into her cup while you listen from yours. Then give your friend a turn. Speak louder and softer to see how well you can hear.
6. Experiment to see how long you can make the string and still hear your friend clearly.

Make sure the string is tight, or the sound waves won't be strong enough to move the string.

When you talk into your cup, the bottom of the cup vibrates. This causes the string to vibrate until it hits the bottom of your friend's cup. These sound vibrations enter your friend's ear, where they can be heard.

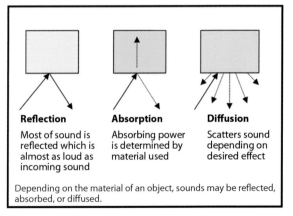

TICK-TOCK REFLECTION

Have you ever been in an auditorium after a band has played or a pep rally has ended? You may have heard a ringing sound. This is caused by sound reflected from the walls and other objects. Sound waves will continue to bounce back and forth until they lose all their energy. Some of a sound wave's energy is absorbed each time it hits an object. The rest is lost as heat.

In an auditorium, it is very important to control this reflection and absorption so that sound can be heard anywhere a person sits. Designers pay special attention to the acoustics of the auditoriums they build. They plan how walls and other surfaces will be angled to reflect sounds to the audience. They also plan materials and surfaces to absorb sounds so there is no echo. The perfect combination and location of reflection and absorption is necessary to an auditorium's success.

Reflection	Absorption	Diffusion
Most of sound is reflected which is almost as loud as incoming sound	Absorbing power is determined by material used	Scatters sound depending on desired effect

Depending on the material of an object, sounds may be reflected, absorbed, or diffused.

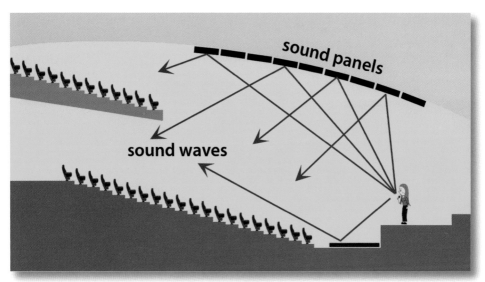

Sound waves from a stage are reflected by sound panels and distributed throughout an auditorium.

In this activity, you will notice the effect of reflection and absorption using some simple household items.

Materials	
◆ 2 cardboard paper towel tubes	◆ Tape
	◆ Ticking clock
◆ Box with a lid	◆ Small piece of cardboard
◆ Scissors	◆ Dishtowel

Instructions

1. Trace a circle on the side of the cardboard box using one of the cardboard tubes.
2. Cut the circle out of the box.
3. Tape one of the tubes in the hole so that it makes a tunnel leading out of the box.
4. Put the ticking clock inside the box and close the lid.
5. Place the other tube at an angle next to the first tube. Put your ear next to the second tube and listen to the clock. Can you hear it?
6. Hold (or have a friend hold) the small piece of cardboard where the ends of the tubes meet. Can you hear the ticking now? Adjust the

cardboard piece until you can hear the ticking of the clock through the tube.

7. Now place a folded dishtowel between the small piece of cardboard and the tube. What happens?

The dishtowel will absorb the sounds coming through the tube.

The sound travels through the first tube and is reflected by the cardboard through the second tube. When you add the dishtowel, the sound is absorbed. Some materials, even though they are solid, absorb sound. Foam, fabric, carpets, and other surfaces with holes are used to absorb sound in places like doctor's offices and libraries. Marble and tile—materials that are commonly used in the lobbies of buildings, reflect sound, creating echoes. Different solids absorb and reflect sounds differently. Try to replace the dishtowel with other materials, such as fabric squares, pieces of wood, a brick, or a piece of Styrofoam, to see which absorb and which reflect sound.

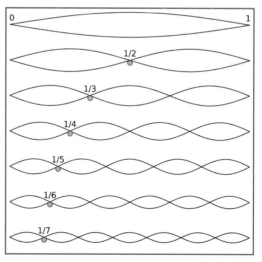

MAKING MUSIC

Some sounds are high, some are low. Some are loud and some are soft. Some are pleasant, some are not. These categories make up three characteristics of sound—pitch, intensity, and quality.

Pitch is how fast sound vibrations are moving. This can be expressed as the number of hertz (Hz), or cycles per minute. The number of Hz represents the frequency of a sound's tone. The higher a sound's frequency is, the higher its pitch.

The intensity of sound is simply its volume. A low tone can be loud or soft, just as a high tone can be. Intensity depends on the strength of the vibration. If the string in a musical instrument (such as a piano) is struck gently, its intensity will be low (soft). If it is struck forcefully, its intensity will be high (loud).

A series of related musical tones creates harmony.

Why do some sounds sound like music and others sound like noise? The answer is sound quality, or timbre. The shriek of an eagle overhead creates a harsh tone—an unpleasant quality. The note coming from a flute is gentle and pleasing. The shape of the waves and how they blend make the difference between a pleasant sound and "noise."

When sounds blend, they are said to harmonize. You can make a harmonic scale using water and drinking glasses.

Materials
- Eight drinking glasses—all the same size and shape
- Water
- Measuring cup
- Spoons
- Several friends

Instructions

1. Set eight glasses on a table in a row.

2. Completely fill one glass with water. Carefully dump the water into a measuring cup. Record, in ounces or milliliters, how much water the glass holds. Divide the number of ounces or milliliters by 16. This will give you the unit to use for adding water to each glass.

Glass	Amount of water, in units
1	1
2	2
3	4
4	6
5	8
6	10
7	12
8	14

3. Fill the first glass with one unit of water. This will be the highest note in the scale.

4. Fill the second glass with two units of water, the third with four units, the fourth with six units, the fifth with eight units, the sixth with ten units, the seventh with twelve units, and the eighth with fourteen units. Each glass will correspond to a note on the musical scale: C, D, E, F, G, A, B, C.

Musical Notes

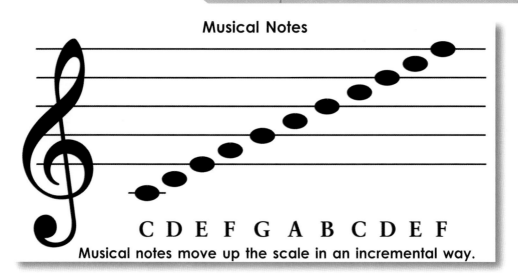

C D E F G A B C D E F

Musical notes move up the scale in an incremental way.

5. Use spoons to gently tap the side of each glass. Can you hear a scale? If a note doesn't sound right, add or take away a little water until it does. (If you have a piano, you can tune your glasses to the piano.)

Keys on a Piano

B C D E F G A B C D E F G A B C

The fuller the glass, the lower the note.

Tap the glasses gently. A light tap will make a clear sound without breaking anything.

Experiment with water levels until you can play a simple song like "Mary Had a Little Lamb."

6. Try hitting two glasses at the same time. Do they harmonize?
7. Next, try rubbing the glasses to create sound. Wet the tip of your finger and rub it around the rim of a glass to make a note. Have two or three friends help by rubbing different glasses at the same time.
8. Have fun trying to make music with your water-glass orchestra!

The pitch changes depending on how fast the glass vibrates. The farther the water goes up the side of the glass, the slower the vibrations and the lower the tone.

F-22 Raptor

SONIC BOOM!

What do fireworks, airplanes, and whips all have in common with you? All these things have the ability to break the sound barrier. The sound barrier is the point where an object moves at the speed of sound. The crack of a whip is one example that can explain this. When you snap your wrist, the wave of motion travels down the whip. As the wave moves, it gathers speed. By the time it reaches the tip of the whip, it is moving faster than the speed of sound. Before the wave reaches the tip, at the point it passes the speed of sound, it creates a shock wave that sounds like a loud crack.

In this activity, you'll build a boomer. This simple paper tool will allow you to break the sound barrier right in your living room. And your parents thought you were loud before you read this book . . .

Materials
- Poster board
- Tracing or wrapping paper
- Scissors
- Tape

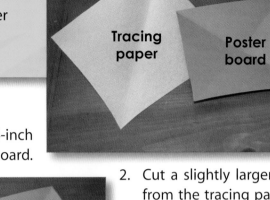

Tracing paper

Poster board

Instructions
1. Cut a 4-inch by 4-inch square of poster board.

2. Cut a slightly larger square from the tracing paper.

3. Cut your tracing paper square in half to make a triangle.

4. Fold the tracing paper over two sides of the poster board and tape into place.

5. Fold the poster board and paper from corner to corner.

6. Hold the corner of your boomer, and fling it downward, making the paper flick out. Get ready for the bang! ➡

The harder you flick your hand, the louder the sound!

Books

Brasch, Nicolas. *Why Does Sound Travel?: All About Sound.* New York: PowerKids, 2010.

Gardner, Robert. *Light, Sound, and Waves Science Fair Projects, Revised and Expanded Using the Scientific Method.* Berkeley Heights, NJ: Enslow Publishers, 2010.

Jankowski, Connie. *All About Light and Sound.* Minneapolis, MN: Compass Point, 2009.

McGregor, Harriet. *Sound.* New York: Windmill, 2011.

Mahaney, Ian F. *Sound Waves.* New York: PowerKids, 2007.

Twist, Clint. *Light and Sound: The Best Start in Science.* Tunbridge Wells, Kent, England: TickTock, 2009.

Works Consulted

Brand, David. "Christopher Clark: Whales off Newfoundland Can Hear Whales near Bermuda." *Cornell Chronicle,* February 24, 2005. http://www.news.cornell.edu/Chronicle/05/2.24.05/AAAS.clark.whales.html

Graham, Sarah. "True Cause of Whip's Crack Uncovered." *Scientific American,* May 28, 2002. http://www.scientificamerican.com/article.cfm?id=true-cause-of-whips-crack

Kids Health from Nemours: Cochlear Implants http://kidshealth.org/parent/general/eyes/cochlear.html#

Luo, Zhexi. "How Whales Hear." Carnegie Museum of Natural History, n.d. http://www.carnegiemuseums.org/cmag/bk_issue/1997/julaug/feat4.htm

NOAA. Ocean Explorer: "Satellites." http://oceanexplorer.noaa.gov/technology/tools/sonar/sonar.html

Pierce, Allan D. *Acoustics, An Introduction to Its Physical Principles and Applications.* Melville, NY: Acoustical Society of America, 1981, 1989. http://acousticalsociety.org/asa_publications/books/01_03_11_pierce.

Russell, Dan, PhD. "Acoustics and Vibration Animations." Flint, MI: Kettering University of Applied Physics, 2002. http://paws.kettering.edu/~drussell/demos.html

White, Ira. *Audio Made Easy: Or How to Be a Sound Engineer Without Really Trying.* Milwaukee, WI: Hal Leonard, 2007.

On the Internet
Kidipede: Sound
http://www.historyforkids.org/scienceforkids/physics/sound/
NASA Science Files Kids: Dr. D's Sound Activities
http://scifiles.larc.nasa.gov/text/kids/D_Lab/acts_sound.html
NDT Resource Center: Reflection of Sound
http://www.ndt-ed.org/EducationResources/HighSchool/Sound/
reflection.htm
NeoK12 Educational Videos, Lessons, and Games for K–12 School Kids:
Sound
http://www.neok12.com/Sound.htm
Zoom Activities for Kids (PBS)
http://pbskids.org/zoom/activities/sci/

Science Supply Companies
Home Science Tools
http://www.hometrainingtools.com/Default.asp?
Science Kit & Boreal Laboratories
http://sciencekit.com/Default.asp?bhcd2=1258230685
Science Kit Store
http://sciencekitstore.com/
Steve Spangler Science Store
http://www.stevespanglerscience.com/

PHOTO CREDITS: Cover—Joe Rasemas; pp. 4, 5, 6, 7, 8, 9, 12, 13, 16, 19, 22, 23 (top), 25, 28, 34, 37—cc-by-sa; pp. 11, 14, 15, 18, 20, 21, 23 (bottom), 24, 26 (bottom), 27, 29, 30, 32, 33, 36, 39 (bottom), 40, 42, 43—Colleen Kessler; pp. 17, 26 (top), 35, 39 (charts)—Sharon Beck; p. 19—U.S. Navy; p. 31—Photos.com/Getty Images; p. 41—U.S. Air Force. Every effort has been made to locate all copyright holders of material used in this book. If any errors or omissions have occurred, corrections will be made in future editions of the book.

acoustics (uh-KOO-stiks)—The study of the physical properties of sound.

amplitude (AM-plih-tood)—The greatest magnitude of a wave.

auditorium (aw-dih-TOR-ee-um)—A room or building designed for lectures, concerts, or other public gatherings.

auricle (AR-ih-kul)—The outer part of the human ear.

cartilage (KAR-tih-lidj)—A strong but stretchy tissue that covers bones and forms the outer ear, end of the nose, and other parts of the body.

cochlea (KOH-klee-uh)—The spiral part of the inner ear that uses fluid and tiny hairs to change sound into electrical signals for the brain.

compression (kum-PREH-shun)—The pushing together of something, making its parts get closer.

cycle (SY-kul)—One complete vibration.

decibel (DEH-suh-bul)—A unit of loudness.

diffraction (dih-FRAK-shun)—The bending of a wave around an object.

echolocation (eh-koh-loh-KAY-shun)—Finding the location of an object by bouncing sound off it and timing how long it takes for the echo to return.

Eustachian tube (yoo-STAY-shun TOOB)—One of the two tubes that connect the middle ear to the throat and control air pressure in the ears.

frequency (FREE-kwen-see)—The number of occurrences in a given time period.

hertz (HERTZ)—The unit used to measure frequency (one cycle per second).

medium (MEE-dee-um)—A substance through which waves can move, such as air, glass, or water.

membrane (MEM-brayn)—A thin layer of tissue (skin) that covers, connects, or separates parts of the body.

period (PEE-ree-ud)—The duration of one cycle of a wave.

pitch (PITCH)—The property of sound that changes along with the frequency of vibration.

rarefaction (rayr-ih-FAK-shun)—The pulling apart of something to spread out its parts.

reflection (ree-FLEK-shun)—Change in direction of a wave after it bounces off an object.

sonar (SOH-nar)—Short for SOund NAvigation and Ranging, the system for using sound to locate objects.

supersonic (SOO-per-sah-nik)—Greater than the speed of sound.

ultrasound (UL-truh-sownd)—The technique that uses very high frequency sound to create images.

vacuum (VAK-yoom)—A space that has no matter in it.

vibration (vy-BRAY-shun)—A shaking motion.

wave (WAYV)—An up-and-down or back-and-forth movement that transfers energy.

wavelength (WAYV-length)—The distance it takes before a wave repeats.

Colleen Kessler is the author of science books for kids, including *A Project Guide to Reptiles and Birds*, *A Project Guide to the Solar System*, and *A Project Guide to Electricity and Magnetism* for Mitchell Lane Publishers. A former teacher of gifted students, Colleen now satisfies her curiosity full-time as a nonfiction writer. She does her researching and writing in her home office overlooking a wooded backyard in Northeastern Ohio. You can often find her blasting off rockets or searching for salamanders with her husband, Brian, and kids, Trevor, Molly, and Logan, or talking to schoolchildren about the excitement of studying science and nature. For more information about her books and presentations, or to schedule her for a school visit, check out her web site at http://www.colleen-kessler.com.